Title Page:

LinkedIn Sales Navigator Guide:

Understanding Digital and Social Selling by Turning Linkedin into Lead, Sales and Marketing

By: Clinton A. Quentin

INTRODUCTION

Many options abound in the realm of sales tools, each with its merits. However, LinkedIn Sales Navigator stands out from the crowd for its unparalleled capabilities in lead generation, prospecting, and lead nurturing.

In today's hyper-connected world, the currency of success isn't just measured in dollars and cents, but in relationships forged and opportunities seized. Whether you're a young professional navigating the early stages of your career or a seasoned financial expert seeking new avenues for growth, the ability to cultivate meaningful connections is paramount. Enter LinkedIn Sales Navigator—a beacon of hope amidst the vast sea of digital networking platforms.

Imagine a tool that not only opens doors but also illuminates the path to your professional aspirations. That tool is LinkedIn Sales Navigator—a compass guiding you through the labyrinth of business landscapes, empowering you to chart your course with precision and purpose.

At its core, LinkedIn Sales Navigator is more than just a platform; it's a catalyst for change, a conduit for transformation. It bridges the gap between ambition and achievement, offering a multitude of benefits tailored to the needs of today's dynamic workforce.

For the youthful dreamer yearning to make their mark on the world, Sales Navigator provides a roadmap to success—one paved with opportunity and lined with possibility. It's a playground of potential where every connection made is a step closer to realizing one's dreams.

And for the seasoned financial expert, Sales Navigator is a strategic ally—a trusted advisor in the pursuit of excellence. It's a treasure trove of insights and intelligence, offering a panoramic view of the market landscape and guiding investment decisions with unparalleled clarity.

But Sales Navigator is more than just a platform—it's a promise. A promise of growth, of opportunity, of prosperity. It's a symphony of human connection, harmonizing the aspirations of individuals with the demands of an ever-evolving marketplace.

So join us on this journey—a journey of discovery, of growth, of transformation. Let LinkedIn Sales Navigator be your guide as we navigate the intricate tapestry of modern business together. Embrace the possibilities, seize the opportunities, and unlock the full potential of your professional destiny.

The future awaits—let's chart our course together.

FOREWARD

The Power of LinkedIn Sales Navigator

Sales Navigator serves as LinkedIn's primary solution for sales professionals, offering a comprehensive suite of tools to support sales representatives, managers, and operations leaders. By leveraging LinkedIn's extensive database, insights, and relationship-building features, Sales Navigator empowers users to refine their sales approaches and strategies effectively.

Imagine, if you will, a world where every connection made is a thread in your professional journey—a world where opportunities abound and possibilities are limitless. This is the world of LinkedIn Sales Navigator—a world where dreams are realized and ambitions are achieved.

LinkedIn Sales Navigator is a testament to the power of human connection. It is a gateway to a vast network of like-minded individuals, each with their own unique stories, experiences, and insights to share. It is a platform where relationships are forged, partnerships are formed, and dreams are brought to life.

But what sets LinkedIn Sales Navigator apart from the rest? It is not just its features or its functionality, but its ability to transcend the mundane and elevate the ordinary to the extraordinary. It is a catalyst for change—a catalyst that propels us forward on our journey to greatness.

For the young entrepreneur with a vision yet to be realized, LinkedIn Sales Navigator offers a roadmap to success—a roadmap paved with opportunity and lined with possibility. It is a guiding light in the darkness, illuminating the path to prosperity and paving the way for a brighter tomorrow.

And for the seasoned professional seeking new horizons to explore, LinkedIn Sales Navigator is a strategic ally—a trusted advisor in the pursuit of excellence. It is a treasure trove of insights and intelligence, offering a panoramic view of the market landscape and guiding investment decisions with unparalleled clarity.

LinkedIn Sales Navigator serves as a dynamic tool for businesses, offering advanced search functionalities and real-time insights to effectively identify and engage with highly qualified leads. Utilizing personalized outreach strategies and content sharing features within Sales Navigator enables professionals to position themselves as authoritative figures in their industries, thereby cultivating trust and attracting valuable leads organically. The seamless integration of Sales Navigator with CRM systems optimizes the lead generation process, preventing missed opportunities and providing invaluable data for refining sales strategies and enhancing overall efficiency.

But perhaps most importantly, LinkedIn Sales Navigator is a testament to the power of community. It is a platform where individuals come together to share ideas, collaborate on projects, and support one another on their journey to success. It is a place where friendships are forged, partnerships are formed, and dreams are brought to life.

If you're seeking a thorough understanding of Sales Navigator's capabilities, functionality, and optimization strategies, you've landed in the right spot. This book equips you with the resources needed to excel in Buyer First Selling, prioritizing the needs and preferences of potential buyers throughout the sales process.

So let us start this journey together—a journey of discovery, of growth, of transformation. Let us harness the power of LinkedIn Sales Navigator to unlock our full potential and forge a brighter future for ourselves and for generations to come.

The power is in our hands—let us wield it wisely.

CHAPTER ONE

Getting Started with LinkedIn Sales Navigator

LinkedIn Sales Navigator stands out as a guiding light—a beacon of opportunity amidst the noise and chaos. We will be explaining what exactly is LinkedIn Sales Navigator, and how can it help you unlock the full potential of your professional network?

What is LinkedIn Sales Navigator?

LinkedIn Sales Navigator is a sophisticated sales tool tailored for virtual selling, facilitating the cultivation and management of buyer relationships on a large scale. Positioned as a cornerstone in the toolkit of contemporary B2B sales teams, Sales Navigator seamlessly integrates with other sales technologies, including CRM systems, to furnish users with a robust repository of up-to-date, trustworthy data.

Regarded as the quintessential LinkedIn iteration for sales professionals, Sales Navigator boasts an array of advanced search functionalities, expanded visibility into extended networks, and personalized algorithms aimed at connecting users with key decision-makers precisely when needed.

Essentially, LinkedIn Sales Navigator is a premium subscription service designed to empower sales professionals, recruiters, and business leaders with advanced tools and insights for navigating the ever-expanding landscape of professional networking. It serves as a turbocharged version of the standard LinkedIn platform, offering enhanced features and functionalities tailored to the needs of individuals who rely on networking and relationship-building for their success.

Sales Navigator's Potential

Sales Navigator serves as a multifaceted tool designed to empower sales professionals in fulfilling three pivotal functions integral to their craft.

Identify: Expedite the process of pinpointing individuals and organizations that align with your product or service offerings, facilitating swift and informed decision-making regarding potential prospects.

Analyze: Stay abreast of significant developments within target accounts, such as shifts in key personnel or signals of buying intent, enabling proactive engagement and timely action on emerging opportunities.

Interact: Foster meaningful connections and conversations with prospects within a conducive business environment, leveraging LinkedIn's extensive messaging and content-sharing functionalities to nurture relationships and drive engagement.

In today's sales landscape, where prioritizing the buyer's needs reigns supreme and virtual interactions have become the norm, Sales Navigator emerges as a crucial tool for sales professionals. By equipping users with valuable insights, enabling differentiation through added value, and facilitating relationship-building essential for customer acquisition, Sales Navigator paves the way for sales success in an evolving marketplace.

Unlocking the Benefits

The benefits of LinkedIn Sales Navigator are manifold, but perhaps its greatest asset lies in its ability to streamline the process of prospecting and lead generation. With advanced search filters and personalized recommendations, Sales Navigator enables users to identify and connect with potential leads and decision-makers more efficiently than ever before. Moreover, its real-time insights and sales alerts keep users informed about key activities and events related to their leads and accounts, empowering them to engage with prospects at the right time with relevant information.

Navigating the Interface

Upon logging into LinkedIn Sales Navigator, users are greeted with a sleek and intuitive interface designed to maximize productivity and streamline workflow. The dashboard provides a comprehensive overview of key metrics and insights, allowing users to track the performance of their outreach efforts and measure the impact of their networking activities. Additionally, the navigation bar offers easy access to essential features such as advanced search, lead recommendations, and InMail messaging, ensuring that users can quickly find what they need and take action with ease.

Exploring Key Features

LinkedIn Sales Navigator boasts a plethora of features designed to enhance the user experience and drive results. From advanced search filters and lead recommendations to InMail messaging and sales alerts, Sales Navigator offers a comprehensive suite of tools for prospecting, engaging, and nurturing relationships with potential leads and clients. Moreover, its seamless integration with CRM platforms and third-party applications enables users to leverage the power of Sales Navigator across their entire sales ecosystem, ensuring a cohesive and efficient workflow.

Setting Up Your Sales Navigator Account

Setting up your LinkedIn Sales Navigator account begins with selecting the appropriate subscription plan that aligns with your business objectives. LinkedIn offers three distinct tiers: Professional, Team, and Enterprise, each tailored to meet varying organizational needs and sales team dynamics.

Choosing the Right Subscription Plan:

Professional: The Professional tier is ideally suited for individual users seeking to enhance their prospecting capabilities. This plan provides access to advanced search filters and personalized lead recommendations, enabling users to efficiently identify and engage with high-quality prospects. It is an excellent option for solo entrepreneurs, independent sales professionals, and small business owners looking to optimize their networking efforts.

Team: The Team tier is designed to facilitate collaboration and teamwork within small to mid-sized sales teams. In addition to the features available in the Professional plan, Team subscribers benefit from enhanced collaboration tools, including CRM integration and shared InMail credits. These features promote seamless communication and coordination among team members, enabling them to collectively leverage the power of Sales Navigator to drive revenue and achieve shared objectives.

Enterprise: The Enterprise tier caters to larger sales teams and organizations with complex sales processes and extensive networking needs. This plan offers all the features available in the Professional and Team tiers, along with additional benefits such as unlimited lead tracking and enhanced customer support. Enterprise subscribers have access to dedicated resources and advanced analytics tools, empowering them to scale their sales efforts and optimize performance across the organization.

Selecting the Right Fit:

When choosing a subscription plan, it's essential to consider factors such as the size of your sales team, the level of collaboration required, and the complexity of your sales processes. By selecting the plan that best aligns with your business goals and objectives, you can maximize the value of LinkedIn Sales Navigator and drive meaningful results for your organization.

Step 1: Access LinkedIn Sales Navigator

Log in to your LinkedIn account.

Navigate to the LinkedIn Sales Navigator page. You can find it by clicking on the "Work" dropdown menu at the top right corner of your LinkedIn homepage and selecting "Sales Navigator" from the list of options.

Step 2: Choose Your Plan

Once you're on the Sales Navigator page, you'll see different subscription plans available. Choose the plan that best fits your needs and budget. LinkedIn usually offers a free trial period for new users, so you can explore the platform before committing to a paid subscription.

Step 3: Complete Your Profile

If you're a new user, you'll need to complete your profile before accessing Sales Navigator. Make sure your LinkedIn profile is up-to-date and includes relevant information about your professional experience, skills, and interests.

Step 4: Accept Terms and Conditions

Before proceeding, review LinkedIn's terms of service and privacy policy. Once you've read and understood them, click on the "Accept" button to continue.

Step 5: Provide Payment Information (If Applicable)

If you've chosen a paid subscription plan, you'll need to provide payment information to complete the signup process. Enter your credit card details or choose an alternative payment method accepted by LinkedIn.

Step 6: Confirm Your Email Address

LinkedIn may require you to confirm your email address to activate your Sales Navigator account. Check your email inbox for a confirmation message from

LinkedIn and follow the instructions provided to verify your email address.

Step 7: Customize Your Preferences

Once your account is set up, take some time to customize your preferences and settings. You can adjust your notification preferences, set up saved searches, and customize your dashboard to suit your needs.

Step 8: Explore Sales Navigator Features

Congratulations! Your LinkedIn Sales Navigator account is now set up and ready to use. Take some time to explore the various features and tools available, such as advanced search filters, lead recommendations, and InMail messaging, to maximize your networking and prospecting efforts.

Navigating the Sales Navigator Interface

Navigating the Sales Navigator interface requires a meticulous approach to fully harness its capabilities. Let's delve into the intricacies of navigating this powerful tool and understanding its key features.

Dashboard Overview:

Upon logging into Sales Navigator, you're greeted with a comprehensive dashboard that serves as your command center. Take a moment to meticulously examine each element of the dashboard, including key metrics, saved searches, and account alerts. Understanding the layout and functionality of the dashboard is crucial for optimizing your workflow and staying informed about relevant activities.

Advanced Search Functionality:

The cornerstone of Sales Navigator lies in its advanced search capabilities, allowing users to meticulously filter and pinpoint their ideal prospects. Take the time to explore the various search filters available, such as company size, industry, and job title, and understand how each parameter can be meticulously tailored to your specific needs. By mastering the art of advanced search, you can navigate through the vast sea of potential leads with precision and purpose.

Lead Recommendations and Insights:

Sales Navigator provides users with meticulously curated lead recommendations and real-time insights into prospect activities. Take advantage of these features to meticulously identify high-potential leads and stay informed about relevant developments within your target accounts. By meticulously analyzing lead recommendations and insights, you can uncover hidden opportunities and tailor your outreach efforts for maximum impact.

InMail Messaging and Engagement:

InMail messaging is a powerful feature of Sales Navigator that allows users to meticulously craft personalized messages and engage with prospects directly. Take a meticulous approach to crafting your InMail messages, ensuring that each communication is tailored to the recipient's interests and needs. By meticulously nurturing relationships through thoughtful engagement, you can establish trust and credibility with your prospects, paving the way for meaningful conversations and potential conversions.

Integration with CRM Systems:

The seamless integration of Sales Navigator with CRM systems offers a meticulously streamlined approach to lead management and data organization. Take the time to meticulously configure the integration settings to ensure smooth data synchronization between Sales Navigator and your CRM platform. By meticulously leveraging this integration, you can meticulously track prospect interactions, monitor pipeline activity, and meticulously optimize your sales strategies for maximum efficiency.

CHAPTER TWO

Optimizing Your Profile for Sales Success

Every sales professional understands the necessity of rest, even amidst pressing deadlines or nearing quota targets. However, the beauty of LinkedIn lies in its ability to serve as your steadfast advocate even while you sleep. A well-optimized LinkedIn profile functions as a dynamic social selling microsite, continually presenting your best self to prospective clients and customers. It becomes a canvas where your personality, skills, and professional mission statement are vividly portrayed, ensuring a compelling representation in the digital realm, day or night. Let's examine how you can maximize the potential of your profile by focusing on crafting compelling content, leveraging premium features, and building a robust network.

Crafting a Compelling LinkedIn Profile:

Crafting a compelling LinkedIn profile is essential for making a lasting impression on potential prospects. Below is how you can optimize your profile:

Professional Headline: Your headline should be concise and attention-grabbing, clearly stating your value proposition or area of expertise.

Summary Section: Use the summary section to provide a compelling overview of your professional background, skills, and achievements. Focus on highlighting your unique selling points and what sets you apart from others in your field.

Experience and Accomplishments: Detail your work experience and key accomplishments in a clear and concise manner. Use bullet points to highlight specific achievements and quantify your impact whenever possible.

Skills and Endorsements: List relevant skills and encourage colleagues and clients to endorse you for those skills. This adds credibility to your profile and reinforces your expertise in your field.

Engaging Media: Incorporate multimedia elements such as videos, presentations, or portfolio samples to showcase your work and provide additional context to your profile visitors.

By crafting a compelling LinkedIn profile, you can effectively communicate your value proposition and establish yourself as a trusted authority in your industry, thereby attracting potential leads and opportunities.

Leveraging LinkedIn Premium Features:
LinkedIn offers a range of premium features that can enhance your profile's visibility and reach. Here are some key features to consider:

InMail Messaging: LinkedIn Premium allows you to send InMail messages to prospects even if you're not connected. Use this feature strategically to reach out to potential leads and initiate meaningful conversations.

Advanced Search Filters: Premium users have access to advanced search filters that allow for more precise targeting of prospects based on criteria such as industry, company size, and seniority level. Utilize these filters to identify and connect with your ideal prospects more effectively.

Profile Views: Premium users can see who has viewed their profile, providing valuable insights into the interest and engagement levels of potential leads. Use this information to prioritize follow-ups and tailor your outreach efforts accordingly.

LinkedIn Learning: Take advantage of LinkedIn Learning courses offered through Premium subscriptions to enhance your skills and stay updated on industry trends. Continuous learning can help you stay ahead of the curve and position yourself as a knowledgeable resource for your prospects.

Building a Strong Network:
Building a strong network of connections is fundamental to sales success on LinkedIn. Here's how you can strategically grow your network:

Connect Strategically: Identify and connect with individuals who are relevant to your industry, target market, or niche. Personalize your connection requests to establish a genuine rapport and increase the likelihood of acceptance.

Engage Actively: Engage with your connections by sharing valuable content, participating in discussions, and offering insights and expertise. Active engagement helps you stay top-of-mind with your network and fosters stronger relationships over time.

Join Groups and Communities: Join LinkedIn groups and communities that are relevant to your industry or interests. Participate in discussions, share insights, and connect with fellow members to expand your network and build credibility within your niche.

Offer Value: Focus on offering value to your network rather than solely promoting your products or services. Share helpful resources, offer advice and assistance, and be genuinely interested in helping others succeed.

Personalizing Your LinkedIn Sales Navigator Account for Optimal Success

Once you've selected the appropriate subscription plan, the next step is to personalize your LinkedIn Sales Navigator account, tailoring it to align with your unique sales preferences and target market. This personalized approach is where the true power of Sales Navigator comes to fruition, allowing you to unlock its full potential and maximize your chances of a successful lead generation campaign.

Embarking on the Journey:
Embarking on the LinkedIn Sales Navigator journey marks the beginning of a transformative experience in your sales endeavors. It's at this post-subscription stage where the real magic happens through personalization, as you fine-tune your account settings to suit your specific needs and objectives.

Personalization Tips for Success:

Here are some essential personalization tips to guide you towards a successful lead generation campaign:

Optimize Your Profile: Start by sprucing up your LinkedIn profile to make a lasting impression on potential leads. Ensure your profile features a professional headshot and a compelling summary that succinctly conveys your professional journey, skills, and aspirations. A polished profile establishes credibility and builds trust with prospects.

Tailor Lead Preferences: Dive into the 'Settings' section of Sales Navigator and meticulously define your lead preferences and account criteria. By setting precise parameters, you ensure that you receive notifications only for leads that align closely with your business goals and target market, streamlining your prospecting efforts and maximizing efficiency.

CRM Integration: Seamlessly integrate Sales Navigator with your CRM software to streamline your lead management process. Syncing your Sales Navigator account with your CRM system eliminates the need for manual data entry and prevents the hassle of juggling between multiple platforms. This integration ensures that all lead information is centralized and easily accessible, allowing for more efficient tracking and follow-up.

Leverage Available Tools: Don't hesitate to explore additional tools and services, especially those related to CRM integration, to enhance your lead management process. Take advantage of available resources to optimize your workflow and make your sales efforts as smooth and efficient as possible.

How to Boost Sales with LinkedIn Sales Navigator

LinkedIn Sales Navigator can be a game-changer for sales professionals, but unlocking its full potential requires a strategic approach. Below are invaluable tips to help you harness the power of this software and elevate your sales performance to new heights.

Enhance Your Profile

Entering the realm of LinkedIn Sales Navigator is undoubtedly thrilling. With its promise to facilitate connections with high-quality leads, close lucrative deals, and boost commissions, the anticipation is palpable.

However, before delving headfirst into the plethora of features designed to crush quotas, it's imperative to tackle a seemingly mundane yet indispensable task: optimizing your profile.

A well-optimized LinkedIn profile serves as the cornerstone of visibility on the platform, laying the groundwork for success in proactive outreach endeavors. To put it simply, a lackluster profile can significantly impede lead generation and prospecting efforts.

Profile optimization is a straightforward process. Begin by investing in a professional headshot, utilize the summary section to articulate the value you bring while strategically incorporating relevant keywords, provide a comprehensive overview of your work experience, and ensure your contact details are easily accessible.

Research indicates that a staggering 82% of buyers conduct LinkedIn searches before engaging with outreach efforts. Therefore, it's prudent to refrain from contacting ideal customers until your profile is impeccably curated.

Define Your Ideal Customer

Understanding your target audience is paramount to sales success.

If you find yourself hesitating for more than a moment when asked, "Who do you sell to?" it's time to refocus. After all, familiarity with this demographic should be second nature.

Once you've gained comprehensive insight into your ideal customer base, heed the professional advice that advocates for the creation of buyer personas. This strategic step enables you to leverage Sales Navigator's advanced search filters effectively, segmenting and pinpointing potential clients based on various pertinent criteria such as industry, job title, seniority level, geographical location, and company size.

Utilize Advanced Search Filters

Once you've identified your target audience, Sales Navigator's search functionality becomes your greatest ally.

The significance of Sales Navigator's advanced search features, highlighting its ability to pinpoint leads matching your Ideal Customer Profile (ICP). By saving these searches, you can curate targeted lists, enabling seamless tracking and engagement with potential customers over time—a topic we'll delve into further in the next tip.

By this, Sales Navigator simplifies the process of refining search criteria with operators like AND, OR, NOT, as well as parentheses and quotes.

For instance, if you're seeking sales managers, simply input "Sales Manager" into Sales Navigator. To broaden your search to include sales or marketing managers, you can use "Sales Manager" OR "Marketing Manager." Moreover, if your aim is to connect directly with CEOs while circumventing gatekeepers, employing a query such as "CEO NOT Assistant" can prove effective.

Thus, this streamlines the search process considerably. The question remains: what's next once you've amassed a trove of leads? The answer lies in creating a lead list—a pivotal step in capitalizing on the opportunities unearthed through your searches.

Compile a Lead Catalog

After defining your search criteria in Sales Navigator, the platform sifts through its vast user base of 930 million professionals to identify those fitting your specifications. However, with such a colossal pool of users on LinkedIn, precision is paramount to avoid drowning in irrelevant leads.

The importance of leveraging Sales Navigator's search filters extensively. While this may result in a smaller list, it ensures a higher quality of prospects tailored to your preferences. Once you've pinpointed leads aligning with your ideal customer profile, it's time to assemble them into a lead list:

1. Choose the desired lead(s)
2. Click the "Save to List" button located below the search bar
3. Select the appropriate list to store the lead(s)

Access all your saved leads through the "Lead Lists" tab within Sales Navigator. From this interface, you can also jot down notes, dispatch connection requests, and send LinkedIn messages to prospects.

Utilize Lead Recommendations

The allure of LinkedIn Sales Navigator is undeniable, but its capabilities extend even further.

The significance of lead recommendations offered by Sales Navigator, which are tailored to your saved leads and sales preferences. These recommendations serve as a valuable resource for discovering new potential customers.

In essence, Sales Navigator analyzes your past searches and prospecting behavior to curate a list of potential leads, streamlining the process of identifying prospects. Imagine the efficiency gained when potential buyers are delivered directly to you, eliminating the need for extensive outreach efforts.

Leverage the TeamLink Functionality

Sales Navigator's TeamLink feature enables sales teams to tap into each other's networks. Why does this matter? Because it significantly simplifies engagement with second-degree connections—LinkedIn users connected to your direct network but not to you. By leveraging this feature, you naturally enhance trust with prospects, ultimately leading to increased sales.

So, how does it operate? Begin by accessing the advanced search feature within your Sales Navigator account. Navigate to the "Spotlights" section, then proceed to click the "Activities and Shared Experiences" button. From there, select the "With TeamLink Into" option in the dropdown menu.

Sales Navigator will then display all prospects connected to your colleagues.

Note: TeamLink functionality is exclusively available to subscribers of the "Advanced" and "Advanced Plus" plans.

Initiate Contact with Your Leads

Once you've compiled a roster of potential customers, it's time to make contact. LinkedIn offers two primary avenues for outreach: connection requests and InMail messages.

A connection request mirrors a friend request on Facebook—it's a request to connect with another LinkedIn user. Conversely, an InMail message is a private message exchanged between LinkedIn users who aren't yet connected.

With your Sales Navigator membership, you're allotted 50 InMails per month. Consequently, it's advisable to begin with connection requests. Should your request go unanswered, then consider utilizing InMail.

Regardless of the method chosen, reference specific elements from their profile, such as shared connections or recent activities. Emphasize the value you bring to the table. Avoid generic templates, striving instead for authenticity in your communication.

Interact with Others' Content

LinkedIn Sales Navigator is not just a stellar tool for lead generation and prospecting—it's also an asset for nurturing leads.

Sales Navigator grants you visibility into the content your prospects share and engage with. Seize this opportunity by engaging with their posts through likes, comments, and shares.

Why is this advantageous? Firstly, it provides invaluable insights into your target audience. Prospects share content that resonates with them, offering a window into their interests and needs. Armed with this knowledge, you can tailor your sales pitches effectively, guiding prospects closer to a purchase.

Furthermore, engaging with potential customers' content helps maintain your presence in their minds. As they see your interactions—likes, comments, and shares—they're reminded of your presence and offerings. This subtle yet consistent engagement nudges them further down your sales funnel.

With a few clicks—liking, commenting, and sharing—you effortlessly advance these prospects along the sales journey. It's a win-win!

Utilize the Smart Links Functionality

Let us take an instance where you have been nurturing a particular lead for weeks. You recognize the potential benefits of your company's product for them, yet you haven't quite clinched the deal. Despite this, they've been receptive to your outreach efforts, engaging in back-and-forth interactions on LinkedIn posts.

Then, out of nowhere, the prospect sends you a LinkedIn message, saying, "I've just embarked on a new project and could really use a product like yours. Can you provide more information?"

This is the moment you've been anticipating. You break into your happy dance, then compose yourself and consider this: why not send them a Smart Link?

A Smart Link is an ingenious feature on LinkedIn that enables Sales Navigator users to compile multiple pieces of content—such as pitch decks, product overviews, and demonstration videos—into one trackable link. This link can then be shared through any preferred channel.

Smart Links streamline content sharing and offer insights into engagement metrics by leveraging data to prioritize follow-ups and tailor your approach to match your prospects' interests.

To clarify, Smart Links empower you to deliver content to prospects, monitor their interactions with the content, and devise effective follow-up strategies based on the collected data. Simply put, Smart Links are a game-changing feature of Sales Navigator that you should integrate into your workflow without delay.

Note: Smart Links are exclusively accessible to subscribers of the "Advanced" and "Advanced Plus" plans.

CHAPTER THREE

Advanced Search Techniques

LinkedIn Sales Navigator revolutionizes the way users search for prospects by offering unparalleled filtering options not available in the basic LinkedIn search functionality. With Sales Navigator's advanced search capabilities, users gain the precision of a seasoned angler, effortlessly pinpointing the most relevant prospects amidst the vast sea of professionals. This dynamic feature serves as a powerful tool, enabling users to fine-tune their outreach efforts with surgical precision.

Exploring Advanced Search Capabilities:

In this section, we be discussing the depth and breadth of Sales Navigator's advanced search capabilities, exploring how they can be a game-changer in your lead generation journey. From filtering by industry, company size, and job title to leveraging sophisticated search parameters like geographic location and seniority level, Sales Navigator offers a comprehensive array of options to refine your search results and identify the most promising leads.

Precision Filtering for Targeted Outreach:

By harnessing Sales Navigator's advanced search capabilities, users can tailor their search criteria to align closely with their ideal customer profile. Whether you're targeting decision-makers in Fortune 500 companies or niche professionals in emerging industries, Sales Navigator empowers you to zero in on the prospects that matter most to your business objectives. This precision filtering not only saves time and resources but also increases the likelihood of engaging with high-quality leads primed for conversion.

Maximizing Efficiency and Effectiveness:

The ability to filter search results with precision transforms the lead generation process, enabling users to streamline their outreach efforts and focus their attention on prospects with the highest potential for conversion. By leveraging Sales Navigator's advanced search capabilities, users can optimize their workflow, prioritize their outreach efforts, and ultimately drive greater ROI from their sales activities.

Utilizing Advanced Search Filters

LinkedIn Sales Navigator's advanced search filters serve as a beacon of precision, empowering users to navigate through the vast sea of potential prospects with unparalleled accuracy. In this section, we'll delve into the intricacies of utilizing advanced search filters and uncover how they can elevate your prospecting game to new heights.

Sales Navigator's advanced search filters offer a wealth of customization options, allowing users to refine their search criteria with surgical precision. From industry and company size to job title and geographic location, these filters enable users to tailor their search queries to align closely with their specific objectives and target audience.

Fine-Tuning Your Search Criteria:

When utilizing advanced search filters, it's essential to consider the nuances of your target market and the unique characteristics of your ideal prospects. Take the time to meticulously refine your search criteria, considering factors such as industry trends, geographic preferences, and buyer personas. By fine-tuning your search parameters, you can ensure that you're targeting prospects who are genuinely relevant to your business goals.

Exploring Custom Search Combinations:

One of the most powerful features of Sales Navigator's advanced search filters is the ability to combine multiple criteria to create highly targeted search queries. Experiment with different combinations of filters to uncover hidden opportunities and identify prospects that meet your specific criteria. Whether you're searching for decision-makers in a particular industry or seeking prospects within a specific geographic region, custom search combinations enable you to tailor your search queries to your unique requirements.

Leveraging Saved Searches for Efficiency:

To streamline your prospecting efforts and save time, consider utilizing the "Saved Searches" feature in Sales Navigator. Once you've configured your ideal search criteria, save the search for future use, allowing you to quickly access relevant prospects with just a few clicks. Saved searches can be customized and refined over time, ensuring that you're always up-to-date with the latest opportunities in your target market.

Generating Targeted Lead Lists

In the realm of sales and business development, success hinges on the ability to identify and engage with high-potential leads effectively. LinkedIn Sales Navigator provides a robust platform for generating targeted lead lists, enabling users to streamline their prospecting efforts and focus their attention on prospects with the greatest potential for conversion. In this section, we'll explore the art and science of crafting targeted lead lists using Sales Navigator's powerful features and tools.

Targeted lead lists are curated collections of prospects that meet specific criteria based on your business objectives and target market. These lists serve as a foundation for your prospecting efforts, providing a roadmap for identifying and engaging with prospects who are most likely to convert into customers or clients. By leveraging Sales Navigator's advanced search capabilities and filtering options, users can tailor their lead lists to align closely with their ideal customer profile and maximize their chances of success.

Defining Your Ideal Customer Profile:

Before embarking on the process of generating targeted lead lists, it's essential to have a clear understanding of your ideal customer profile. Consider factors such as industry, company size, geographic location, and job title when defining your criteria. By articulating your ideal customer profile upfront, you can ensure that your lead lists are finely tuned to meet your specific requirements and objectives.

Utilizing Advanced Search Filters:

Sales Navigator offers a wide range of advanced search filters that allow users to refine their search criteria with precision. From industry and company attributes to job function and seniority level, these filters enable users to narrow down their search results and identify prospects that closely match their ideal customer profile. By strategically combining multiple filters, users can create highly targeted lead lists tailored to their unique requirements.

Leveraging Lead Recommendations and Insights:

In addition to advanced search filters, Sales Navigator provides users with personalized lead recommendations and real-time insights into prospect activities. These features offer valuable guidance and intelligence for identifying new opportunities and prioritizing engagement efforts. By leveraging lead recommendations and insights, users can supplement their targeted lead lists with additional prospects who may not have appeared in their initial search results, further expanding their pool of potential leads.

Organizing and Managing Lead Lists:

Once you've generated your targeted lead lists, it's essential to organize and manage them effectively within Sales Navigator. Utilize features such as tags, notes, and custom lists to categorize and prioritize your leads based on factors such as stage of engagement, level of interest, and potential value. By maintaining a well-organized lead database, you can ensure that you stay focused and efficient in your prospecting efforts, maximizing your chances of success.

Finding Decision-Makers and Influencers

In the intricate landscape of business development, success often hinges on the ability to connect with decision-makers and influencers who hold the key to unlocking valuable opportunities. LinkedIn Sales Navigator serves as a powerful tool for identifying and engaging with these pivotal figures, allowing users to navigate through the digital maze of professionals with precision and purpose. In this section, we'll explore the strategies and techniques for finding decision-makers and influencers using Sales Navigator's advanced features and functionalities. Decision-makers and influencers are individuals within an organization who wield significant authority and influence over key business decisions. These individuals may occupy various roles, including C-level executives, department heads, team leaders, and industry thought leaders. Identifying and connecting with decision-makers and influencers is essential for gaining access to valuable opportunities and driving meaningful outcomes in sales and business development initiatives.

Utilizing Advanced Search Filters:

Sales Navigator offers a diverse range of advanced search filters that enable users to pinpoint decision-makers and influencers with precision. Leveraging filters such as job function, seniority level, and company size, users can narrow down their search results to focus exclusively on individuals who hold decision-making authority or wield significant influence within their organizations. By strategically combining multiple filters, users can create highly targeted lists of decision-makers and influencers tailored to their specific objectives and target market.

Leveraging TeamLink Connections:

TeamLink Connections is a unique feature of Sales Navigator that allows users to leverage their team's network connections to identify decision-makers and influencers within target organizations. By tapping into the collective network of their colleagues and teammates, users can uncover valuable insights and introductions that may not be accessible through traditional search methods. TeamLink Connections facilitate warm introductions and mutual connections, increasing the likelihood of engaging with decision-makers and influencers effectively.

Exploring Lead Recommendations and Insights:

In addition to advanced search filters, Sales Navigator provides users with personalized lead recommendations and real-time insights into prospect activities. These features offer valuable guidance for identifying decision-makers and influencers based on their engagement patterns and interactions within the LinkedIn ecosystem. By leveraging lead recommendations and insights, users can uncover hidden opportunities and prioritize engagement efforts with individuals who are most likely to drive meaningful outcomes for their business.

Engaging Thoughtfully and Strategically:

Once decision-makers and influencers have been identified, it's essential to engage with them thoughtfully and strategically. Personalized messaging, relevant content sharing, and mutual connections can help establish rapport and credibility, paving the way for meaningful conversations and potential collaborations. By approaching interactions with decision-makers and influencers with authenticity and professionalism, users can build valuable relationships that lead to mutually beneficial outcomes.

CHAPTER FOUR

Leveraging Insights and Recommendations

In the dynamic landscape of professional networking, LinkedIn has emerged as a cornerstone platform for professionals worldwide to connect, network, and expand their business horizons. Boasting a staggering user base of over 700 million individuals, LinkedIn presents an abundance of opportunities for lead generation, prospecting, and relationship cultivation. However, navigating this vast digital terrain efficiently can prove to be a formidable challenge for many. This is precisely where Sales Navigator steps in – a purpose-built tool meticulously crafted to empower businesses and individuals alike to harness the full potential of LinkedIn.

In today's digital age, the strategic utilization of social media platforms for business growth is no longer just an option – it's a necessity. LinkedIn, as the premier professional network globally, stands out by offering unparalleled avenues for professionals to showcase their expertise, forge meaningful relationships, and cultivate lucrative leads. Whether you're an entrepreneur seeking new opportunities, a sales professional looking to expand your client base, or a thought leader aiming to establish industry credibility, LinkedIn provides the ideal platform to amplify your presence and achieve your business objectives.

Using Lead Recommendations Effectively

In the realm of sales and business development, strategic insights and targeted recommendations can be the catalysts for unlocking untapped opportunities and driving tangible results. LinkedIn Sales Navigator, with its arsenal of advanced features, offers users a treasure trove of insights and lead recommendations to propel their prospecting efforts to new heights. In this section, we'll explore the art of leveraging these invaluable resources effectively, with a focus on maximizing the potential of lead recommendations.

Sales Navigator provides users with real-time insights into prospect activities, engagement patterns, and relevant industry trends. These insights offer valuable intelligence to inform decision-making and guide strategic outreach efforts. By staying abreast of prospect behavior and market dynamics, users can tailor their approach, anticipate needs, and position themselves as trusted advisors in their respective fields.

Unlocking the Potential of Lead Recommendations:

One of the most powerful features of Sales Navigator is its personalized lead recommendations, which are curated based on user preferences, past interactions, and LinkedIn's proprietary algorithms. These recommendations serve as a goldmine of potential leads, offering users a curated list of prospects who match their ideal customer profile. By leveraging lead recommendations effectively, users can uncover new opportunities, expand their network, and accelerate their sales pipeline with precision and efficiency.

Strategies for Effective Utilization:

To make the most of lead recommendations on Sales Navigator, consider the following strategies:

Regularly Review Recommendations: Set aside dedicated time to review lead recommendations on a regular basis. LinkedIn continuously updates its recommendations based on user activity and changes in the market landscape, so staying vigilant ensures you don't miss out on valuable opportunities.

Refine Your Preferences: Take advantage of Sales Navigator's customization options to refine your lead preferences and fine-tune your recommendations. Adjust filters such as industry, company size, and geographic location to ensure that recommendations align closely with your target market and business objectives.

Engage Thoughtfully: When reaching out to leads recommended by Sales Navigator, personalize your messages and engage thoughtfully. Reference shared interests or mutual connections to establish rapport and demonstrate genuine interest in building a meaningful relationship. A personalized approach fosters trust and increases the likelihood of a positive response.

Track and Measure Results: Monitor the effectiveness of your outreach efforts to leads recommended by Sales Navigator. Track metrics such as response rates, conversion rates, and pipeline velocity to gauge the impact of your activities and identify areas for improvement. Use this data to refine your approach and optimize your prospecting strategy over time.

Harnessing Real-Time Insights for Engagement

In the dynamic landscape of sales and relationship-building, timely and informed engagement is key to cultivating meaningful connections and driving successful outcomes. LinkedIn Sales Navigator offers a wealth of real-time insights that can serve as invaluable resources for guiding strategic outreach efforts and fostering productive interactions. In this section, we'll explore how to harness these insights effectively to enhance engagement and optimize your sales efforts.

The Power of Real-Time Insights:

Sales Navigator provides users with a rich array of real-time insights, including updates on prospect activities, changes in company dynamics, and relevant industry trends. These insights offer a window into the evolving needs and priorities of your target audience, empowering you to tailor your outreach efforts accordingly and engage with prospects in a timely and relevant manner.

Strategies for Leveraging Real-Time Insights:

To maximize the impact of real-time insights in Sales Navigator, consider implementing the following strategies:

Stay Informed: Regularly monitor updates and alerts in Sales Navigator to stay informed about changes in prospect behavior, company news, and industry developments. Pay attention to signals such as job changes, promotions, and content engagement to identify opportunities for meaningful engagement.

Customize Your Outreach: Use real-time insights to personalize your outreach efforts and tailor your messaging to align with prospect interests and needs. Reference recent activities or relevant news articles in your communications to demonstrate attentiveness and relevance, increasing the likelihood of engagement.

Seize Opportune Moments: Capitalize on timely opportunities identified through real-time insights to initiate conversations and nurture relationships. Whether it's congratulating a prospect on a recent promotion or sharing insights relevant to their industry, seize the moment to demonstrate your value and establish rapport.

Adapt and Iterate: Continuously monitor the effectiveness of your engagement efforts and adjust your approach based on real-time feedback and performance metrics. Analyze engagement data, such as response rates and conversion rates, to identify trends and patterns that inform future outreach strategies.

Benefits of Real-Time Engagement:
Engaging with prospects in real-time offers several benefits, including:

Enhanced Relevance: By aligning your outreach efforts with current events and prospect activities, you demonstrate relevance and increase the likelihood of capturing their attention.

Increased Responsiveness: Real-time engagement allows you to seize opportunities as they arise, enabling prompt responses and fostering a sense of urgency in your interactions.

Strengthened Relationships: By demonstrating attentiveness and responsiveness through real-time engagement, you build trust and credibility with prospects, laying the foundation for long-term relationships and future collaborations.

Staying Updated with Sales Alerts

In the fast-paced world of sales, staying updated with the latest developments and opportunities is paramount to success. LinkedIn Sales Navigator provides a powerful feature known as Sales Alerts, designed to keep users informed about critical changes and activities within their network. In this section, we'll explore how to leverage Sales Alerts effectively to stay ahead of the curve and capitalize on timely opportunities.

Sales Alerts in Sales Navigator are real-time notifications that alert users to important updates and activities related to their leads and accounts. These alerts cover a wide range of events, including job changes, company news, content engagement, and more. By receiving timely alerts about key developments within their network, users can identify opportunities, anticipate needs, and take proactive steps to engage with prospects and clients effectively.

Strategies for Maximizing Sales Alerts:
To make the most of Sales Alerts in Sales Navigator, consider implementing the following strategies:

Customize Your Alerts: Tailor your Sales Alerts to focus on the most relevant and impactful events for your sales objectives. Customize alert settings based on criteria such as lead status, industry, and geographic location to ensure that you receive notifications that align with your target market and business goals.

Prioritize Your Follow-Up: Act swiftly on Sales Alerts to capitalize on timely opportunities and engage with prospects when their interest is at its peak. Prioritize your follow-up efforts based on the urgency and significance of the alert, focusing on prospects who are most likely to benefit from immediate attention.

Personalize Your Outreach: Use Sales Alerts as conversation starters to personalize your outreach efforts and demonstrate attentiveness to prospect activities. Reference recent events or achievements mentioned in the alert to establish rapport and relevance, increasing the likelihood of engagement and response.

Stay Organized: Keep track of Sales Alerts and follow-up actions using Sales Navigator's built-in tools, such as tags, notes, and reminders. Organize your alerts systematically to ensure that no opportunity falls through the cracks and that you stay on top of your sales pipeline effectively.

Benefits of Using Sales Alerts:

Timely Opportunity Identification: Sales Alerts enable users to identify and capitalize on timely opportunities within their network, allowing them to stay ahead of the competition and seize valuable prospects and clients.

Enhanced Engagement: By acting on Sales Alerts promptly, users can engage with prospects when their interest is at its peak, increasing the likelihood of meaningful interactions and successful outcomes.

Proactive Relationship Management: Sales Alerts empower users to take proactive steps to nurture relationships and address potential risks or challenges before they escalate, fostering trust and loyalty with clients and prospects alike.

Engaging with Prospects: Crafting Personalized InMail

In the realm of modern sales and business development, personalized communication is the cornerstone of building meaningful relationships and driving successful outcomes. LinkedIn Sales Navigator offers a powerful tool known as InMail, which allows users to send direct messages to prospects, even if they're not connected. In this section, we'll explore strategies for crafting personalized InMail messages that resonate with prospects and foster productive engagements.

Understanding the Power of Personalization:
Personalization is key to capturing the attention and interest of prospects in today's digital age. Generic, one-size-fits-all messages are quickly dismissed, while personalized communications that speak directly to the recipient's needs and interests are more likely to elicit a positive

response. By tailoring your InMail messages to address the specific concerns and objectives of each prospect, you demonstrate attentiveness and relevance, increasing the likelihood of engagement and conversion.

Strategies for Crafting Personalized InMail Messages:

To maximize the effectiveness of your InMail messages in Sales Navigator, consider implementing the following strategies:

Research and Segmentation: Take the time to research each prospect thoroughly and segment your target audience based on relevant criteria such as industry, job function, and interests. This allows you to tailor your messages to resonate with the unique needs and preferences of each segment, increasing the relevance and impact of your communications.

Personalized Greeting: Start your InMail message with a personalized greeting that addresses the recipient by name and acknowledges any shared connections or common interests. This sets a friendly and welcoming tone and demonstrates that you've taken the time to research and personalize your message.

Highlight Mutual Benefits: Clearly articulate the value proposition of your message and how it aligns with the recipient's objectives and challenges. Focus on the benefits that your product or service can offer and how it can help the recipient achieve their goals or overcome specific pain points.

Call to Action: Include a clear and compelling call to action that prompts the recipient to take the next step, whether it's scheduling a meeting, requesting more information, or downloading a resource. Make it easy for the recipient to respond by providing clear instructions and contact information.

Follow-Up Plan: Anticipate potential objections or questions from the recipient and proactively address them in your message. Offer to provide additional information or address any concerns they may have, and outline your follow-up plan to keep the conversation moving forward.

Benefits of Personalized InMail Messages:

Increased Response Rates: Personalized InMail messages are more likely to capture the attention and interest of recipients, leading to higher response rates and engagement levels.

Improved Relationship Building: By demonstrating attentiveness and relevance in your communications, you lay the foundation for building stronger relationships with prospects over time.

Enhanced Brand Perception: Personalized messages convey professionalism and authenticity, enhancing the recipient's perception of your brand and increasing their willingness to engage with you further.

CHAPTER FIVE

Best Practices and Tips for Successes

Harnessing Sales Navigator for Seamless Sales Team Integration

First of all, to harness seamless sales, effective collaboration is the linchpin of success. LinkedIn Sales Navigator offers a suite of features designed to facilitate seamless collaboration among sales teams, enabling them to leverage collective insights, share resources, and coordinate efforts for maximum impact. In this section, we'll explore strategies for harnessing Sales Navigator to foster collaboration and integration within your sales team.

Sales Navigator provides sales teams with a centralized platform to share valuable insights, coordinate outreach efforts, and align strategies for optimal results. By collaborating effectively within Sales Navigator, teams can leverage collective knowledge and expertise to identify opportunities, nurture relationships, and drive successful outcomes.

Strategies for Collaborating with Sales Teams: To maximize the benefits of team collaboration in Sales Navigator, consider implementing the following strategies:

Shared Lead Lists: Create shared lead lists within Sales Navigator to centralize prospecting efforts and ensure visibility across the team. Collaboratively curate lists of high-potential leads, segment them based on relevant criteria, and assign ownership to individual team members for follow-up.

TeamLink Connections: Leverage TeamLink Connections to tap into the collective network of your sales team and identify mutual connections with prospects. By leveraging shared connections, you can facilitate warm introductions, establish credibility, and accelerate the sales process.

CRM Integration: Integrate Sales Navigator with your CRM system to streamline lead management and ensure seamless communication between platforms. Syncing data between Sales Navigator and your CRM allows team members to access up-to-date information, track interactions, and coordinate follow-up activities more effectively.

Collaborative Messaging: Use Sales Navigator's messaging features to facilitate collaborative communication within your sales team. Share insights, exchange best practices, and coordinate outreach efforts through group messages and threads, enabling team members to collaborate in real-time and stay aligned on strategy.

Benefits of Team Collaboration in Sales Navigator:

Enhanced Visibility: Collaborating within Sales Navigator provides visibility into team activities, progress, and results, enabling better coordination and alignment of efforts.

Improved Efficiency: By centralizing prospecting efforts and sharing resources, sales teams can work more efficiently, reduce duplication of efforts, and maximize productivity.

Collective Intelligence: Leveraging the collective knowledge and expertise of the sales team enables better decision-making, informed strategies, and more effective engagement with prospects and clients.

Integrating Sales Navigator with CRM Tools

the integration of LinkedIn Sales Navigator with Customer Relationship Management (CRM) tools offers a potent combination for driving sales effectiveness and maximizing productivity. By bridging the gap between prospecting and pipeline management, this integration empowers sales teams to seamlessly leverage insights from Sales Navigator within their existing CRM workflows. In this section, we'll explore the strategies and benefits of integrating Sales Navigator with CRM tools.

The integration of Sales Navigator with CRM tools enables sales professionals to access valuable insights and prospect data directly within their CRM platform. This seamless connection streamlines lead management, enhances visibility into prospect interactions, and facilitates more informed decision-making throughout the sales process. By uniting these two powerful tools, sales teams can leverage the best of both worlds to drive efficiency and effectiveness in their sales efforts.

Strategies for Integration:
To maximize the benefits of integrating Sales Navigator with CRM tools, consider implementing the following strategies:

Select the Right CRM Platform: Choose a CRM platform that offers robust integration capabilities with Sales Navigator, ensuring compatibility and seamless data synchronization. Popular CRM systems such as Salesforce, Microsoft Dynamics 365, and HubSpot CRM offer native integrations with Sales Navigator, making it easy to connect the two platforms and leverage their combined capabilities.

Sync Prospect Data: Configure the integration to sync prospect data, including profile information, activity history, and engagement metrics, between Sales Navigator and your CRM platform. This ensures that sales teams have access to up-to-date prospect information within their CRM system, eliminating the need for manual data entry and ensuring data consistency across platforms.

Automate Workflows: Leverage automation capabilities to streamline sales workflows and eliminate repetitive tasks. Set up automated processes to capture new leads from Sales Navigator, assign them to the appropriate sales representatives, and track their progress through the sales pipeline. Automation reduces administrative overhead and frees up time for sales teams to focus on high-value activities.

Utilize Sales Navigator Insights: Take advantage of Sales Navigator's insights and recommendations to inform sales strategies and prioritize prospect engagement. Integrate these insights into your CRM workflows to provide sales teams with valuable context and guidance for their outreach efforts, enabling them to make more informed decisions and drive more effective interactions with prospects.

Benefits of Integration:

Enhanced Visibility: Integration with CRM tools provides sales teams with a comprehensive view of prospect interactions and engagement metrics, enabling better-informed decision-making and more targeted outreach.

Improved Efficiency: Streamlining lead management and automating workflows reduces manual effort and administrative overhead, allowing sales teams to focus their time and energy on activities that drive results.

Seamless Collaboration: Integration fosters seamless collaboration between sales and marketing teams by aligning prospect data and insights across departments, enabling more coordinated and effective sales strategies.

Setting and Tracking Sales Navigator Goals

setting clear goals and tracking progress is essential for driving meaningful results and maximizing return on investment (ROI). LinkedIn Sales Navigator offers a wealth of features and functionalities designed to support sales professionals in achieving their objectives. By establishing and monitoring specific goals within Sales Navigator, sales teams can measure success, optimize performance, and demonstrate the value of their efforts. In this section, we'll explore strategies for setting and tracking Sales Navigator goals effectively.

Setting SMART Goals:

Before diving into goal tracking, it's crucial to establish clear and actionable goals that align with your sales objectives. Utilize the SMART criteria to ensure your goals are Specific, Measurable, Achievable, Relevant, and Time-bound. For example, a SMART goal for Sales

Navigator might be to increase the number of qualified leads generated by 20% within the next quarter through targeted prospecting and outreach.

Key Performance Indicators (KPIs) for Sales Navigator:

Identify the key performance indicators (KPIs) that will enable you to measure progress towards your goals within Sales Navigator. Some common KPIs for Sales Navigator include:

Lead Generation: Measure the number of qualified leads generated through Sales Navigator outreach efforts.

Engagement Metrics: Track metrics such as InMail response rates, connection acceptance rates, and profile views to gauge prospect engagement.

Pipeline Velocity: Monitor the progression of Sales Navigator leads through the sales pipeline and track conversion rates at each stage.

Opportunity Creation: Measure the number of opportunities created as a result of Sales Navigator activities, such as booked meetings or product demos.

Utilizing Sales Navigator Reporting Tools: Sales Navigator offers reporting tools and analytics dashboards that provide insights into key performance metrics and trends over time. Leverage these tools to track progress towards your goals, identify areas for improvement, and make data-driven decisions to optimize your sales efforts.

Regular Performance Reviews: Schedule regular performance reviews to assess progress towards your Sales Navigator goals and make adjustments as needed. Use these reviews as an opportunity to analyze performance metrics, celebrate successes, and identify areas for improvement. Collaborate with team members to share best practices, troubleshoot challenges, and set action plans for achieving future goals.

ROI Analysis:

Conduct a comprehensive ROI analysis to evaluate the effectiveness of your Sales Navigator efforts and quantify the impact on business outcomes. Compare the cost of Sales Navigator subscriptions and associated expenses against the tangible benefits and revenue generated from Sales Navigator activities. Use this analysis to demonstrate the ROI of Sales Navigator to key stakeholders and justify ongoing investment in the platform.

Continuous Optimization:

Iterate and refine your Sales Navigator strategy based on insights gathered from goal tracking, performance reviews, and ROI analysis. Continuously experiment with different tactics, messaging strategies, and targeting criteria to optimize results and maximize ROI over time.

Analyzing Performance Metrics

data-driven decision-making is paramount for achieving success and maximizing return on investment (ROI). LinkedIn Sales Navigator offers a wealth of performance metrics and analytics tools that enable sales professionals to measure the effectiveness of their efforts and optimize their strategies for optimal results. In this section, we'll delve into the process of analyzing performance metrics in Sales Navigator to drive success and ROI.

Identifying Key Performance Metrics:

Before diving into analysis, it's crucial to identify the key performance metrics (KPIs) that align with your sales objectives and reflect the impact of your Sales Navigator activities. Some common KPIs to consider include:

Lead Generation: Measure the number of qualified leads generated through Sales Navigator outreach efforts.

Engagement Metrics: Track metrics such as response rates to InMail messages, connection acceptance rates, and profile views to gauge prospect engagement.

Pipeline Velocity: Monitor the progression of Sales Navigator leads through the sales pipeline and track conversion rates at each stage.

Opportunity Creation: Measure the number of opportunities created as a result of Sales Navigator activities, such as booked meetings or product demos.

Utilizing Sales Navigator Analytics:
Sales Navigator provides robust analytics tools and reporting dashboards that enable users to track and analyze performance metrics over time. Leverage these tools to gain insights into the effectiveness of your Sales Navigator activities,

identify trends and patterns, and make informed decisions to optimize your sales efforts.

Segmenting Data for Deeper Insights:

To gain deeper insights into your Sales Navigator performance, consider segmenting your data based on various criteria such as industry, job function, geographic location, or engagement level. By analyzing performance metrics across different segments, you can identify high-performing segments, target areas for improvement, and tailor your outreach strategies accordingly.

Comparing Performance Against Benchmarks:

Benchmarking your performance against industry standards or internal benchmarks can provide valuable context for evaluating your Sales Navigator efforts. Compare your performance metrics against relevant benchmarks to assess your relative performance, identify areas of strength and weakness, and set realistic goals for improvement.

Iterating and Optimizing Strategies:

Based on your analysis of performance metrics, iterate and optimize your Sales Navigator strategies to maximize results and ROI. Experiment with different tactics, messaging strategies, and targeting criteria to identify what works best for your target audience. Continuously monitor performance metrics and adjust your strategies accordingly to drive continuous improvement.

Demonstrating ROI:

Finally, use your analysis of performance metrics to quantify the ROI of your Sales Navigator activities and justify ongoing investment in the platform. Calculate the cost of Sales Navigator subscriptions and associated expenses against the tangible benefits and revenue generated from

Sales Navigator activities to demonstrate the ROI to key stakeholders.

Dos and Don'ts of Using Sales Navigator

LinkedIn Sales Navigator is a powerful tool for sales professionals, offering a wide range of features to enhance prospecting, relationship-building, and lead generation. To maximize the effectiveness of Sales Navigator and achieve your sales objectives, it's essential to follow best practices and avoid common pitfalls. Here are some dos and don'ts to keep in mind when using Sales Navigator:

Dos:

Define Your Ideal Customer Profile (ICP): Clearly define your ideal customer profile to ensure you're targeting the right prospects. Use Sales Navigator's advanced search filters to narrow down your search criteria and identify high-quality leads that match your ICP.

Personalize Your Outreach: Personalization is key to successful prospecting. Tailor your messages to each prospect's needs and interests, referencing relevant details from their profile or recent activities to demonstrate your attentiveness and relevance.

Engage Thoughtfully: Focus on building relationships rather than making immediate sales pitches. Engage with prospects thoughtfully by sharing valuable content, offering insights or advice, and seeking to understand their challenges and objectives.

Utilize TeamLink Connections: Leverage TeamLink Connections to tap into your team's network and identify mutual connections with prospects. Warm introductions from shared connections can significantly increase your chances of success.

Track and Measure Results: Use Sales Navigator's analytics tools to track key performance metrics such as lead generation, engagement rates, and pipeline velocity. Continuously monitor your results and adjust your strategy based on insights from your data.

Don'ts:

Send Generic Messages: Avoid sending generic or spammy messages to prospects. Personalization is essential for building rapport and trust, so take the time to craft thoughtful, relevant messages that resonate with each individual recipient.

Overlook Privacy Settings: Respect the privacy settings of your prospects and avoid sending connection requests or messages to individuals who have explicitly indicated they prefer not to be contacted.

Neglect Relationship Building: Don't focus solely on making immediate sales. Building relationships takes time and effort, so invest in nurturing connections over the long term rather than pursuing quick wins.

Ignore Social Selling Etiquette: Be mindful of social selling etiquette when engaging with prospects on LinkedIn. Avoid aggressive sales tactics, spamming, or excessive self-promotion, as these can damage your reputation and credibility.

Neglect Training and Education: Don't overlook the importance of training and education when using Sales Navigator. Take advantage of available resources such as tutorials, webinars, and online courses to deepen your understanding of the platform and maximize its potential.

If all these dos and don'ts are duly followed, you can enhance your prospecting efforts, build stronger relationships with leads, and ultimately drive greater success in your sales initiatives. With a strategic approach and a focus on best practices, Sales Navigator can become a valuable asset for achieving your sales objectives and driving meaningful results in your business.

Proven Strategies from Industry Experts

Industry experts have honed strategies and techniques for leveraging LinkedIn Sales Navigator to achieve remarkable success. By studying and implementing these proven strategies, sales professionals can elevate their prospecting efforts, strengthen relationships, and drive meaningful results. Here are some insights from industry experts on maximizing success with Sales Navigator:

Targeted Prospecting: Industry experts emphasize the importance of targeted prospecting to identify and engage with high-quality leads. By defining clear Ideal Customer Profiles (ICPs) and using Sales Navigator's advanced search filters, sales professionals can narrow down their search criteria and focus their efforts on prospects that align with their target audience.

Personalized Outreach: Personalization is a cornerstone of effective prospecting on Sales Navigator. Industry experts recommend tailoring outreach messages to each individual prospect, referencing relevant details from their profile or recent activities to demonstrate attentiveness and relevance. Personalized messages are more likely to resonate with recipients and elicit a positive response.

Engagement Strategies: Building meaningful relationships with prospects requires thoughtful engagement strategies. Industry experts advocate for a mix of content sharing, insightful comments, and personalized messages to nurture connections and establish rapport over time. By providing value and demonstrating expertise, sales professionals can position themselves as trusted advisors and thought leaders in their industry.

Utilizing TeamLink Connections: Leveraging TeamLink Connections is a key strategy recommended by industry experts for expanding your network and gaining access to warm introductions. By tapping into your team's collective network, you can identify mutual connections with prospects and request introductions from shared connections, increasing your chances of success.

Tracking and Measuring Results: Industry experts stress the importance of tracking and measuring key performance metrics to gauge the effectiveness of Sales Navigator efforts. By monitoring metrics such as lead generation, engagement rates, and pipeline velocity, sales professionals can identify areas of strength and weakness and make data-driven decisions to optimize their strategies for success.

Continuous Learning and Improvement: Finally, industry experts emphasize the importance of continuous learning and improvement when using Sales Navigator. Sales professionals should stay updated on best practices, attend training sessions or webinars offered by LinkedIn, and seek guidance from industry peers to enhance their skills and stay ahead of the curve.

By incorporating these proven strategies from industry experts into their Sales Navigator approach, sales professionals can unlock the platform's full potential and achieve remarkable success in their prospecting and business development efforts. With a strategic mindset, personalized approach, and commitment to continuous improvement, Sales Navigator can become a powerful asset for driving growth, generating leads, and achieving sales objectives in any industry.

CONCLUSION

So far so good, the future of LinkedIn Sales Navigator shines brightly with promise and possibility. With technology advancing at an unprecedented pace and consumer behaviors evolving rapidly, staying ahead of the curve has never been more crucial. Let us embark on a journey of anticipation and preparedness, guided by insights and fueled by innovation.

Predictions for the Future of LinkedIn Sales Navigator:

As days go and time pass, LinkedIn Sales Navigator is envisioned as an indispensable tool for sales professionals. With advancements in artificial intelligence and machine learning, Sales Navigator will become increasingly adept at delivering personalized insights, predicting buyer behavior, and facilitating deeper connections between professionals. Enhanced integrations with CRM systems and other sales tools will streamline workflows and empower sales teams to work more efficiently and collaboratively than ever before.

Staying Ahead of the Curve:

In a world of constant change and disruption, the key to success lies in our ability to adapt and innovate. By embracing change with open arms and embracing a mindset of continuous learning and improvement, we can position ourselves to thrive in any environment. Let us embrace new technologies, explore emerging trends, and challenge ourselves to push the boundaries of what is possible. With Sales Navigator as our compass, we can navigate the winds of change with confidence and chart a course towards success.

Final Words of Encouragement:

Thus, let us remember that the road ahead may be fraught with challenges, but it is also filled with opportunities. Let us approach each obstacle as a chance to learn and grow, each setback as a stepping stone towards greater achievements. With determination in our hearts and resilience in our spirits, we can overcome any obstacle and achieve our wildest dreams. Together, we can forge a path towards a brighter, more prosperous future.

Next Steps for Continued Growth:
As we bid farewell to the present and set our sights on the horizon, let us commit ourselves to taking action towards our goals. Let us leverage the power of Sales Navigator to its fullest potential, harnessing its capabilities to drive growth, generate leads, and achieve success. Let us embrace change as an opportunity for growth and innovation, and let us never stop striving to reach new heights of excellence. The journey ahead may be challenging, but with Sales Navigator as our guide, the possibilities are endless.

In conclusion, let us march forward with confidence, courage, and conviction. With Sales Navigator as our compass, we can navigate the uncertainties of tomorrow with grace and determination, knowing that the future holds boundless opportunities for those who dare to seize them. Let us embrace the journey ahead with open hearts and open minds, ready to embrace whatever the future may bring.

www.ingramcontent.com/pod-product-compliance
Lightning Source LLC
Chambersburg PA
CBHW070305230526
45470CB00002B/726